Diary of a
Motorcycle Babe

Diary of a Motorcycle Babe

Carmen V. Stern

authorHOUSE®

AuthorHouse™
1663 Liberty Drive
Bloomington, IN 47403
www.authorhouse.com
Phone: 1-800-839-8640

First published by AuthorHouse   07/09/2011

ISBN: 978-1-4634-3037-5 (sc)
ISBN: 978-1-4634-3036-8 (ebk)

Printed in the United States of America

This Book is Dedicated to:

My Husband Dale

For his gentle patience in teaching me to learn how to drive a motorcycle properly and his enthusiasm in the journey's between driving and dancing.

My Dance Students

For sharing your fears about
learning to dance
and
Allowing me to share my fears about
learning to drive

Barry

Remember what I said . . .
If I can do it . . .
You can do it.

FORWARD

For Christmas my husband gave me a motorcycle trike. This was a wish that I had made many many years before I met him but which I felt would never really come to pass.

I was never really into motorcycles, but when I saw this Trike in the store, I fell in love with it and I just knew that it was something I would love to have and be able to ride and handle.

There were a couple of things that I did not see on the Trike at the time . . . you know . . . little stuff . . . like the clutch and the gear thing on the foot and I also never really considered that perhaps my hands might be too small to reach and squeeze such a clutch thing or something ridiculous like that! I was too caught up in what a gorgeous machine it was and how much fun it would be to own and ride one.

So that was my wish back seven years ago and now I had it. We got delivery of the Trike in Feb and I began to study the DMV booklet to take the test for the permit.

Let the story begin . . . .

March 14, 2011

I went for permit test to get endorsement for motorcycle trike. I studied the booklet for two weeks before.

Cinch . . . .

I Failed.

March 15—Failed
March 16—Failed
March 17—Failed
March 22—Failed
March 23—Failed
March 24—I passed! Woooo Hooo!

March 25

I had my first "sitting" lesson sitting on the trike. Dale explained all the gizmos and gadgets. The mere size of the Trike is overwhelming. He had me do all the movements on a "cold" bike. Brake in, key on, clutch in, find neutral, etc, etc, etc . . .

He did this exercise with me over and over again and each time I managed to do it differently. I knew what I needed to do, but it never materialized that way in the actual execution. It was most frustrating to me not to be able to keep the sequence right.

By the time this exercise was over I was in tears and wanted and hoped for a way out. I admitted defeat and could hardly swallow the enormous slice of humble pie that I had nearly choked on. Dale would not let me back out and however, and I feared that I would be a blank page again the next day. I was.

March 27

Lesson One—Going forward & learning gears

Today was an excellent day for grinding gears, lunging and lurching forward and back, stalling, jerking and sputtering in perfect order immediately after going into first gear and never making it 10 feet forward. This poor trike will be falling apart before I am ever capable to really drive.

March 28

Lesson Two—Same as lesson one. Maybe a little less lurching and jerking . . . . um . . . . well . . . on second thought, maybe not. I'm trying really hard to feel the shift of the pull in the clutch as I go from 1st gear to 2nd. Dale said I did good . . . but I warned him that I'm an instructor too and I know "exactly what he means!"

March 30

Lesson Three—Same as lesson one. Maybe just a hair better than 2 days ago . . . . but not much. The scary part is getting on the trike and going blank at the very beginning. Trying just to remember the sequence of the "start up". I think maybe if I was 30 years younger, that the sequence might be sticking by now, but, I know me and I know at the age of 58 . . . . it's going to take a lot of staring at the controls when I first get on to get going. The funny thing is I don't remember anything else that I've ever done in life to be harder. This is absolutely THE HARDEST challenge I have ever EVER had in my life. I must conquer! I must conquer.

I can understand how my dance students feel. The beginners. The first lesson is overwhelming to them as I am giving them a host of things they need to remember. I see their panic as their brain goes into overload mode and I chuckle to myself because I'm thinking it can't be so difficult. Now, God has chosen to show me just how they feel and the way that I will see what they are going thru is to be a total beginner myself and to go thru the same brain overload.

I know things start to calm down for a dance student after the first 4 weeks. Basically they have taken 4 lessons and hopefully have practiced during the week. If they have then each lesson is a little better than the last. If they have not, then there is the torture of having to reteach the lesson.

So I'm thinking . . . what is the equivalent of my 4 hours of lesson teaching to my lesson learning? I mean, how long will it take me to get to that level of their 4 weeks? Is it the same? Of course I'm asking this question and today was only day 3 of driving stop and go. I'll revisit this question again in 4 weeks.

My biggest fear is that my margin of error is zero. You can't just "sort of stop" at a light. You have to really stop. Then what about the corners where you don't have to stop and Dale says keep going . . . . give it gas . . . . and . . . and . . . I want to slow down!!!

My lesson for the day was coming to a fast stop. If I could only stop the bike with the look of terror on my face! The look of absolute terror on my face is enough stop ANYTHING dead in its tracks. Unfortunately, it's NOT enough to stop the bike.

I have visions of coming to a complete halt and doing a somersault in the air as I send Dale flying past me overhead. Once more I'm in overload. Time to go home.

April 1

Today was a beautiful day for driving. As we set out for my practice session, that fear starts creeping in as I am locking the house door. By the time I get to the trike I'm already nervous. It's not like you get in the car and you put your foot on the brake and turn on the key. Well, hmmm . . . maybe it is but I'll tell you . . . don't argue with me because it's not that feeling. No.

As soon as I'm on the trike: I begin the mental count of my steps. Let's see now . . . Foot on brake . . . key on . . . clutch in . . . look for neutral . . . clutch out . . . press start switch . . . clutch in . . . shift to first . . . release brake . . . let out the clutch slowly while I roll on the throttle . . . and go!! Aha! You say!

She's got it! No. I don't. I had to correct myself even as I was writing this. I'm still sorting this procedure in my head and it's no easier each time I start from the beginning. It's coming but it's not a natural thing yet, this procedure.

So we head out to the practice streets and I'm finding that today it's just a teeny tiny itsie bitsy bit better than it was last session.

I'm beginning to feel the clutch a little better and I'm doing a little better at not just dropping the clutch. So maybe I only dropped it 80% of the time today.

I was also a little better at using my brakes today. Good thing, huh? The last session I braked and came to a full stop in the middle of the street.

Thank God for small residential streets!

Dale tried to trick me a couple of times to get me to turn right at corners that were part of a bigger street, but I only had to do that once to remember not to go there again. I will. I will . . . but not yet. I need to learn to deal with the little or no traffic first. Preferably the no traffic as I'm still getting to know the trike and it's power.

Today was definitely a better day. My first day was a —zero and on a scale of 1 to 10. 10 being the best . . . I finally made it to 1 today.

Scary moments came when I encountered police cars. Three of them. The first was at the corner that Dale tried to trick me on. I was supposed to turn right and there he was on my right hand side. It was somewhat unnerving. The second car a while later came from my left as I was stopped and waiting to turn right again and then the last was right in front of me as I crossed over one big intersection so I could get to our neighborhood. That was SCARY. There is no getting to my neighborhood without crossing that light which is like 6 lanes wide.

I really felt like I made progress today even though I only got to 1, but believe me . . . 1 is good.

At the end of 90 minutes we went home for lunch. Do you know how it felt? All these days on the trike have felt like I'm on a bucking bronco, lunging and lurching and then finally, I start to get the feel for the clutch and the beast starts to calm down, so that when I get home it says to me . . . . ok . . . you did good . . . I'll let you wash me now. It was a nice feeling. I was starting to feel a bond and connection to my mo-car (that's what I call my trike).

So I rinsed it off, washed it a little, waxed it and polished it up and made it look all pretty and went in for lunch. I was excited for the next trip out after lunch. We would do another hour then.

I learned during the second trip out that I'm not as fresh as the first round and also just more tired. So therefore my one went back down to zero during the second trip out for the day. Once again I was back to lurching and lunging and killing the engine.

Arrrrgh!!!

April 2

Today was not a good day. Too windy and a COLD wind at that. Yesterday was 76 degrees and today as 55! Anyway, I got off to a bad start. Killed the engine on a left turn, consecutively three times, making the driver in the car behind me mad and honking his horn and yelling obscenities at me as he passed around. I sat there for still another five minutes (and this is just on a residential street). I saw the man pass me as he yelled along the way and then I saw him turn left again at the next corner which was not far off and stop. He sat there continuing to watch me from afar as I still sat there, rattled at this point, trying to concentrate and go forward. I could not get back to the business at hand as I could see that he was sitting there just watching and then he came back again and passed in front of me. I finally got the gear thing right and made my left turn. I went off into the other streets as Dale directed and eventually came back to where I saw the man last. He passed me and gave me a look. I know that he had no clue that I am a novice driver, but I wondered if it never crossed his mind that maybe the reason I did not just take off at the corner was because I am just a baby driver in learning mode. I wanted to wear a safety vest that says student driver, but Dale said no. Why not? It would not embarrass me any. In fact I think it would help to keep drivers like that jerk off my back end. Oh well. Dale still said no.

That kind of set the tone for today and between that happening first off and the cold and cold wind, I was not doing too well. I did learn one new thing though. I learned how to go from stop to start a little more smoothly by giving it gas first as I release the clutch. Up until now I had been doing it backwards . . . releasing the clutch first and trying to give it gas, which caused me to lurch a lot. So this left a little better. I think I'm back to killing the engine but I think I will do better tomorrow. A fresh start. Today was not the day.

Another thing I learned today was to keep warmer clothes in the trike. After yesterday's warm weather, I went out today without a sweater under my coat. I could feel the wind creeping in from all directions. Not fun. Skill level today. One.

April 3

Dear God, Thank you for the motorcycle. I know I wanted it. You know I wanted it. Next time I want something I should probably not have; remind me of this time. What was I thinking!?

I don't feel that I got off to a good start today. We broke the session into two parts. Part one was only a repetition of yesterday, but after we stopped to get gas half way through, the second half of my time seemed better. Notice I said seemed, not was. The second half of my session seemed better.

As soon as I got home I headed back out in the car to Office Max. I had an idea. This would be my security blanket! I created a sign and had it laminated for the back of the Trike. The sign said:

> # BACK OFF !!
> # STUDENT DRIVER

The sign itself was a loud iridescent yellow-lime color and the letters big and black! A second smaller sign read "BACK OFF"!

I get nervous when I get to a corner and I'm sitting there trying to figure out what to do and when and how and I'm going thru the whole process in my head for the umpteenth time and in the meantime; someone is sitting right behind me waiting for me to get my act together . . . not realizing that I would go if I could remember what to do or dealing with the fear of "throttle on—clutch off" without lunging forward. Just getting those two things straightened out in my head and able to make the smooth transition is going to take some time. Hopefully not so long.

I think I'll feel better from now on knowing that whoever comes up behind me has a big warning sign staring them in the face that says BACK OFF—Student Driver. They have been forewarned and can either pass around me while I figure out my situation or they can sit there and be patient while I jerk and sputter a few times.

At least now, if someone has the mentality to honk at me I won't feel bad at all. They have options upon reading the warning sign. In the meantime I will continue to do my best not to kill the engine or lunge out. I'll keep doing my best to make my starting transitions nice and smooth.

Every lesson on this trike, is one more lesson which helps me to understand my dance students better as well. But I must do what I tell my students to do. Practice every day.

At the end of April we are signed up to take the safety motorcycle course for Trikes in Yakima, WA. I had these horrible visions of getting over there and not being able to even get the trike started. I'll continue to practice EVERY day this month, so I won't be the worst student there. My rating for the day. Still a 1.

April 4

Why am I writing this book? I am not a pessimistic person, but I guess I am just too impatient with myself. I believe, today is day 7 of my lessons and I'm still trying to get lesson One down.

It's not the actual driving I'm having problems with. It's the starting points. I think I am getting better at my stops, mainly because I'm so cautious. But I think it's that overly cautiousness that is causing my fear on my starts from first gear into second. I don't like the way I lunge and jerk forward.

I suppose I could check in with you every so often and write when things are really happening, but then, you would miss the REAL emotions and real feelings of the moment. I guess when I finally do get to that point where I graduate to level 2, I want you to be with me in my journey. It's kind of like having the reader on the back seat of my trike. You are probably having thoughts of your own, as you make this journey with me.

I'm not sure how long it will take me to reach my goal, but I hope you will still be with me for the ride so we can celebrate the end of this book together.

I got my Motorcycle Book for Idiots today. I should get the Motorcycle book for Dummies tomorrow. I'm off to read.

April 5

My fibromyalgia was hurting too much to go out practicing today. I spent my time reading from my two dummy books. We'll see about tomorrow.

April 6

Too windy and too cold. We went out but came back in after 5 minutes. So windy I could hardly breathe.

April 9

After a couple of days of cold and windy weather, we finally got back on the practice today. I worked on my stops and starts today and I felt like I went back on track. I was not jerking as much and my starts were a little smoother. I'm still at a one but with a couple more days like today, I think I may graduate up a notch to a two. I was able to do 90 minutes today and the time went faster. I think that is a good sign.

April 10

Today Dale pushed me out of the nest! He's leaving to Seattle tomorrow to visit his mother and will be gone for 4 days. That's 4 days that I won't get to practice . . . . unless . . . . unless I do it myself . . . .

So when I got out there this morning, he had a plan already in his head. He sent me off on my own to go around the block. It was scary, but when I got back a few minutes later, I felt like I could do it again on my own. So I asked for another go and still a third. I did it!

I also felt like my start from stop position has improved ever so slightly. My homework is to practice driving around the neighborhood working on my own with my starts and stops.

After I got back from my third round, we went over to the neighborhood that has lots of streets that are good for practicing.

I would say that my rating has gone from a 1 to a 1.5

I will practice this week while he is gone.

April 12

I went out on my own today. I practiced for an hour and went around and around the neighborhood. I practiced shifting from 1st to 2nd and sometimes 3rd gear. I practiced my left turns and right turns and for the time being; I treated all my stops as complete stops so that I could practice my starts and getting the feel of the throttle with one hand as I release the clutch with the other. I think I did a little better today.

To me the trike feels like a beast that I must tame and keep control of. A wild stallion that is ready to rear and roar if I don't watch it. So I drive very carefully and like a little old lady. (LOL and that's not far from the truth!)

After an hour I noticed that the gas was starting to get low. I contemplated driving out of my neighborhood to the gas station but in order to do that I would have to go on one busy street. I thought about it for a while. If I did not get gas, I would not be able to drive for the next 2 days while Dale is gone, so I better do something. I had a stroke of genius! I took the trike home, put it in the garage and then grabbed my gas can and got in the car and off I went. I came home with 2 gallons of gas. By the time I got back and got the gas in, I was starting to get tired and still had my list of chores that I needed to get started with so I called it a day. Now I have gas and I'll be at it again tomorrow.

I did feel a little better about my neighborhood romp today. I am actually looking forward to tomorrow's practice. I hope it does not rain. I'm not going anywhere if it rains.

After I got back from Home Depot later with the car I decided to look at what kind of street route I could start practicing on that would involve a little jaunt on a regular street but that I could practice on. I found one and I think a couple more days or riding around in the neighborhood on my own and I will be ready to go further out. I think today was the first day since I started that I felt a little better. I'm out there on my own and making the decisions about stopping and starting and turns. I think another 3 days of practice like this and I will be at a 2!

April 14

Today I really surprised myself. Got in gear to go and my initial take off was S-M-O-O-T-H. I heard the words "wow" leave my lips and I amazed myself. Truly. Truly. It's probably no great feat, but I felt one step further in my progress. Dale would have been proud of me. I can't wait to tell him.

So once again, I rode around and around on the 3 streets around our neighborhood. Our "safe" streets. Left turns, right turns. Full stops at the stop signs and navigating 2nd gear turns at others. I even did three different emergency stops at different times and those were okay. I'm not sure what is a good emergency stop. I think I'll have to ask Dale to do one while I'm on the back so I can feel it and experience what the trike does when it's done correctly. Yes. That's a good idea.

After riding around for the hour, I felt confident enough to go to one of the 4 way stops that leads to a semi-full street (Yelm) that I could do a right turn on and right turn again onto our side street where our house is. I felt I could do that much without getting myself into a predicament. Yelm can be busy at certain times of the day or it can be busy only as the light changes and traffic is added from 395 onto Yelm. I felt I could do it and I decided to try it.

The first time felt scary a little. The second time was not too bad. The third and fourth time I felt I could do it from then on. I gave myself a pat on the back and I felt I was closer to moving up a notch. Dale would certainly be happy to hear this AND the fact that my stops and starts were improving.

When I came home I had the feeling that I really would like to try the new loop. The one I charted out by car earlier this week. If it was not for the fact that I am still scared to cross over Hwy 395 to get to my starting point and also I'm not sure if I'm allowed to be out on big streets practicing by myself without my instructor . . . I would have tried it.

I'll have to wait till Dale gets home tomorrow. The funny thing is I really feel like I would like to try this. I remember only a couple of weeks ago, being terrified of getting on the trike and my hour lesson feeling like a 4 hour lesson. I guess this is a good sign, looking forward to going out. I really am looking forward to my next session.

April 15

TWO!!!!!!!! I have reached level TWO!!!! Wooooo Hooooo!!!!

Today I was ready to go out there and do the larger loop. This loop started at our home; went down to the Columbia River on Canal Street and then looped to the right towards old Kennewick, a right turn on Fruitland and then another right turn on Kennewick Ave to bring me back towards home from the other end. I did it!

There was only one problem that made me feel unsure. It started to rain! With no windshield wipers; all the rain is beaded up all over the windshield and then all over my face shield as well. It was difficult to see where I was driving. Difficult to see where any pot holes may be and it felt messy. Okay, I think I just made a decision here. I'm going to be a fair weather driver. Sunshine, nice weather . . . you know . . . like a Cadillac Cruiser! Yeah!!! That's the ticket! I could not wait to get home to wipe my Mo-car (motorcycle car) as I like to call it dry.

But let's get back to that TWO!!! I did it. I drove in REAL streets and I was able to do the gear shift changes from 2nd to 3rd and even 4th. Because of the rain, we only completed one loop. I would have really enjoyed doing the loop 4 or 5 times, but it was not meant to be today. But that's okay. I did it and the only thing I did not like was the rain. But I did it. I have made it to level TWO!!!

I think I will be happy to do the next two weeks of this loop. It's big enough but not a major type street. I would call it manageable and diversified enough. A couple of weeks of this and that will almost bring us up to the three day weekend course of the National Motorcycle Safety Course. At least when we get to this course I won't feel like a total idiot and I will be there with a general understanding of the brakes, clutch and gear, etc.

Dale was really proud of me today. He said I have progresses and I really am at level two. Wow. That's all I can say. Level Two. Wow!

April 17

We got out there today and ran a couple of errands on the trike before starting but it was cold and the wind was way too cold that I could not even concentrate. It started to rain and I could not see where I was going. This was too scary and I cut it short. We went home.

April 18

Today was a 4 loop day. Every time there is a gap of more than one day I feel like I'm starting all over again! It was not a bad driving day but I'm wondering when it will feel like fun. Right now my fear is in the way of any fun.

April 19

Another 4 loop day. Yesterday I pulled a muscle in my left shoulder blade and it was still sore today. Add to that my normal stress of handling the trike and I was like a rigid statue on the trike.

As long as I don't have a lot of other traffic around me, it is giving me a chance to getting used to the road. I say that and at the same time I remind you that the loop I have chosen is not a 'real' busy road. There is so much that I have to be aware of that I might take for granted when driving a regular car.

Dear God . . . this is one of those times I wish you had said NO!

I completed my 4 loops but I was stiff coming in. Muscle aches and the whole nine yards.

The weekend for the Safety Course is about 10 days away. I wonder what the other people who are taking the course are like. I wonder if there will be any women? Women on Trikes? Women my age? My age???? Dear God!!! What was I thinking!?!?!? In another few weeks I'll be 59!!! The first time I had wished and wanted this Trike was when I turned 50. I'm getting a late start, and the thing is (just like I tell my dance students) if you don't use it . . . . you will lose it! What does that mean for me??? I'll have to keep driving my Trike every day whether I feel like it or not . . . or I will lose it!!

The other thing I keep telling my dance students is . . . Stop thinking negatively! Believe me . . . I'm challenging myself on that one . . . I'm really trying. But on the days when my Fibromyalgia is stronger than others; those days are the hardest to think positive.

Tomorrow will be a better day. Tomorrow will be a better day.

April 20

Today was a good day. It must have been my Fibromyalgia yesterday because I felt I did so poorly. Today really was a good day. I did 3 loops AND I went on 2 large arterials. Main streets. We went all the way from old Kennewick to the Columbia Mall area and looped around. I felt much better today than I did yesterday.

We also stopped and I got a pair of REAL motorcycle gloves. Ohhhh they fit nice! Real difference!

If it's not raining tomorrow, we will expand our loop to include the new area which has more traffic.

April 21

Today was an OK day. It was colder and windier than yesterday. I felt like I did better yesterday. I started with 2 loops and then we went on to do the big arterial loop. I had a couple of flubs. Nothing serious but enough that I felt like I went down rather than up.

I think some of the things that are I fear are that of the idiot drivers who will jump out in front of you or turn in front of you when you have the right of way. The jerks who even though they see the huge sign on the back of the trike that says "back off" they come up right behind you and are totally oblivious to the fact that you may roll back or suddenly kill the engine. Students DO do that! I have not in a while, but there is always that fear.

You know, there are some days when I think, Dear God, what the heck am I doing learning to drive a motorcycle at age almost 59! But then there are other days when I really feel jazzed and it does not seem like such a mountainous task.

I am still constantly checking my gears and trying to remember what gear I'm in and the position of my left foot, ready to shift up or down.

April 22

Today was another OK day.
Tomorrow will be better.
3 loops and 1 arterial

I'm embarrassed to tell Dale that my hands hurt after the practice. I do everything I can to stretch my fingers around the clutch. He thinks I'm letting the clutch slip, I'm not. The clutch is slipping on its own, because my fingers are too short to grip as far as they can when the clutch is open all the way. I don't know how to begin to explain this to him.

April 24

Dear Reader, don't be bored. This is supposed to be a diary, remember? The good, the bad and the ugly.

So today was not ugly and not bad. Must have been good! Dale says I have reached level 2 in my quest. There are still so many little issues to address.

April 26

Dale says I've reached level three. That's what he thinks. I still feel like level two.

Today was very windy and a cold wind. It's taking the warm spring days forever to get here. Unseasonably cold they say.

Ten degrees under the norm. Add to that my Fibro pain today and I felt I did poorly. I'm glad Dale has faith in me.

I did my first two loops and then heading to my large arterial ride.

I have a dance student who likes to face the mirror at class. If I change his starting position . . . . he panics. It's amusing to watch, but he finds every way to get back to facing the mirror. That is his comfort zone. Turned in any other position is like instantly forgetting what he is supposed to do next. I REALLY understand that feeling now!

I understand that because today for my large arterial instead of turning right for my start and making right turns all the way around in order to come back; Dale had me make a left start so that all my turns would be left instead. In other words I would be driving my arterial in reverse. Instead of driving it clockwise I would be going counterclockwise.

It's funny because they were the same streets, but they felt totally different to me because I was driving them from a different direction. I understand how my dance students feel and the sense of panic I see on their faces.

I am three days away from my official safety training session. I am happy I can now stop and start, but afraid of the unknown. While my trike is a beauty but under my legs and butt, she feels like a BEAST!

April 27

Never go shopping for noise filters. You better sit down for this one.

Our practice routine began in its normal way. It was a good day. I did 2 loops and 1 main arterial exercise and I did better than yesterday. I really felt like a level 3 today. I think that I could have gone an extra round of arterial today but it was cold and windy again and so that was enough. It's probably just as well, because my hands were hurting by the time we ended.

I feel that I'm improving but for every time I have a good day, I feel the price I pay is in my hands and the Fibro which hurts in my hands.

Well, we came home, changed clothes and headed back out with the car to run some errands. One of which was to stop at the motorcycle store to see if we could find some in-line noise filters for our helmets. I don't know where the noise comes from, but it's some kind of buzzing sound like a bad radio connection. Dale says it drives him crazy. I guess I have been so concentrated on my driving that I block out all noise, except for the sound of the changing gears. We stopped at the motorcycle shop to see if they had something that would filter that buzzing sort of sound.

While Dale was talking with the guy in parts dept. I wandered off to look at all the different motorcycles and such. I came upon the Can-Am Spyder Limited Edition 2011 Roadster in glistening white. In case you are not familiar with this motorcycle . . . it's the one that has 2 wheels in the front and 1 in the back. It has a very futuristic look about it. Space agey for sure.

I've never really thought much about it, other than the fact that it was kind of odd looking in a backward sort of way. You know . . . the reverse from the trike.

While I was standing there looking at it, one of the salesmen came over to me and we exchanged a few comments about it. It was a beautiful machine, no doubt, but to me, still odd looking. I told him that I had just gotten a trike for Christmas and that I was happy with it but that I was still having a hard time adjusting to the clutch and gears and that I was not sure how long it would take me to get that down.

To that he replied "Well, the nice thing about the Spyder is that it does not have a clutch or a gear shift lever for the foot." He instantly had my attention. What??? No clutch??? No gear shift lever?? "So how does it work then?" He showed me a button on the left handlebar and said that just by pressing the button it would shift gears up and down. All I had to do was press the button with my thumb. OMG!!! "No way! You are kidding!" "No" he said " . . . and you don't have to use any gear pedals with your left foot either. As you can see there is nothing there to push with your foot. All you do is use your thumb to gear up or down and this model will even gear down automatically if you don't want to do it yourself."

I stood there just amazed thinking . . . . wow . . . how nice it would be if only my trike had that feature.

The salesman went on. "Another feature on this model is that you don't have two brakes. There is just one brake for all three wheels and it is your right foot brake."

I looked and sure enough there was no hand brake. Just the one foot brake. Suddenly, I was seeing this motorcycle through new eyes.

Dale finally finished his business with the parts dept. and came over to get me. I showed him the cool features on this Spyder and amazingly he did not know this before.

At that point, the salesman started to break it down and tell us about ALL the details of the motorcycle. It was one amazing fact after another and then he opened the front of the Trike and pulled out a huge suitcase. He had me at "no clutch" but after one amazing thing after another, I really was looking at this machine through different eyes.

Dale asked all the usual questions and finally we thanked the man and went home.

We were only down the road when Dale said to me "You know, I would be willing to trade in my motorcycle for that one."

"You would? You really like it?"

Dale asked me if I liked it. "Yeah, it's pretty cool. Especially the no clutch to gear shift pedal and only 1 brake."

"Would you be willing to trade in your new trike for that model?"

I was surprised at myself, how quickly I agreed and said yes.

We got home and I made lunch. While we ate we checked on the computer to see if we could find any other deals on the same motorcycle. We did not. In fact we found out that in the Tri Cities there had been only one other sold recently and this was the only other available one in the Tri Cities. We called Seattle and they did not have them.

The price, 28,099.00

Dale did some computations and we prepared to go back and take a test drive. We also checked blue book prices for his motorcycle and my trike in the event we would trade them in and work a deal. He had paid $18,000 for my trike and the minimum amount that he would take would be $15,000 on a trade in.

So we went back. I'm sure the guys knew we were hooked when they saw us coming back.

Dale took the motorcycle out for a test drive on their huge empty practice lot and I watched. It was amazing to see him on it.

Once again Dale thanked the man and we came home to think again. Within a short time, we took my trike and went back for the third time so they could give us a price for it as a trade in.

It was better than we expected. The man offered $16,000 and he was honest about Dale's Yamaha Ventura. As beautiful as it was he told him he'd be better off to sell it private. He'd get more for it. But he did give us a good price and an additional $1,000 bonus.

So, we went to the motorcycle shop for noise filters and came home with a brand new Can-Am Spyder Limited Edition 2011 Roadster in glistening white. Right off the show room floor with only three miles on it.

We felt we made a good purchase and not a single bit of remorse.

The scary thing is that in two days we will go to the motorcycle safety course and I feel like I'm back to square one now. I will have only tomorrow to get familiar with this motorcycle before the course begins and I'm freaked out!

I told Dale, "Oh well . . . as long as one of us passes the course. I guess that's all that matters!" I'll tell you what, with only one day to prepare for the course with this new motorcycle, it will be nothing short of a miracle if I pass the course.

April 28

OH MY GOSH!!!! I did it!!! Pass GO, Collect $200 and go directly to level FIVE!!! FIVE!!! FIVE!!!

It was so exciting. I cannot begin to tell you! I was scared to death when I got on it. I thought to myself that I would be starting again from square one.

We were able to go to the big lot where Dale got to test drive it and I had my turn there. At first I throttled gingerly as I felt the power under me and after a few rounds, a huge smile came on my face and I felt real joy for the first time. I realized that I had not felt that with my trike. I kept waiting for things to get easier and for the fun feeling to begin but it never did. I had some good days but more harder days than good and I came home exhausted each time. I was never going to progress and be and feel as proficient as I did today. It was amazing!

After a few rounds in this lot I knew I was ready to go. Dale drove us back to my starting point and then it was my turn. As soon as I did a couple of small loops around my neighborhood, I felt I was ready to take on the bigger loop and I was going at a speed I had never dared before . . . . 35 and 40!!

I finished my big loop and told Dale I was ready for my arterial loop and off we went. We stopped on the way and had lunch and then off we went.

And then I did it . . . . I told Dale I was ready to take on the big Boulevard . . . and I did it!! Woooooo Hooooo!!

Suddenly after all this time of spitting and sputtering and jerking and killing the engine, I was driving around corners and stops and starts as smooth as pudding and my confidence level soared 1,000%. Dale was cheering me on from behind me and I did everything right! I really did everything right! I was sooooo excited.

How could it be so difficult with my trike and not only that but to come home on top of that and have my hands aching all the way up to my elbows sometimes. Obviously, the trike was not meant for me. It was not the answer.

I came home so energized today. No pain, no stiffness, and I felt happy, motivated, excited and like I REALLLLLY made progress. Ha Ha!! I'm a level FIVE!!!

Tonight we will pack our bags and tomorrow we will head to Yakima, Washington for our 3 day course in safety driving. And guess what? I feel confident and I am ready! I can't wait. I'm so excited.

April 29

We finally arrived to the weekend of our safety course!

It was a hard day to say the least and nothing to do with the course.

We decided that instead of going by freeway that we would take a secondary highway. It was nice in the way that the driving felt free and the road was ours but we fought the wind for the entire 2 hours of the way. Dale drove for the whole trip and I could see that he was exhausted by the time we reached our destination.

A long 2 hours later we reached the hotel and took our gear in. We had stopped along the route for bathroom break and to eat lunch.

We unpacked our gear and headed out the door to find where the "classroom" was and after that we found a large church parking lot where I practiced going around and around and then I took off from there back on to the real streets to head back to the hotel. It was a nice ride and I felt confident about the driving that I was doing in an unfamiliar area. We got back to the hotel and rested for a while.

Dale went across the street to the Wal-Mart and bought some snacks and something to drink for tonight and tomorrow . . . snack type foods to take with us.

Finally, it was time for the first class, which would be just classroom from 6 to 9 tonight. I won't bore you with the details except to say that we were disappointed with the presentation of the class for the money that we paid. I expected an organized presentation where we would learn important information. What we encountered instead was something that we could have learned from reading the booklet from the DMV. We really hoped that the hands on part of the class would be better.

The class finished just before 9pm and we took off to find a MacDonald's for a quick burger and then back to the hotel. We also realized that Dale had not packed warm enough clothes and he needed an extra sweater or sweatshirt to wear under his jacket. We needed to be at the driving range at 7am and Dale needed something more under his jacket.

Fortunately, the Wal-Mart across the street from the hotel was there to solve our problem. We went there and stopped at the indoor burger place and then went to find a fleece sweatshirt and a thermal under shirt.

The wind had not let up all day and now it was almost 9:30pm and it was still cold and windy. We rushed back to the motorcycle to get our helmets on and get home.

Oh no!!!! Dale had put our helmets in the front compartment of the bike and apparently it must have been a snug fit when he put the lid to close because now he could not get the lid open!!!

We were there for 15 minutes while he tried to unjam the front trunk. I was having visions of us having to cancel the rest of class because we had no helmets and I was having visions of us having to take a bus home because we could not drive without helmets.

Somehow, Dale finessed the hood and got it open and boy were glad.

We got back to the hotel and too tired to do the hot tub that we had planned or anything else, we came in and called it a night.

We must be up at 5am tomorrow for a full day on the course.

April 30

I am happy to say that after a full day of driving instruction on the driving range that Dale and I both agree, I have reached a competency level of 6!

The day was spent doing drills on the huge driving range. I did ovals and figure eights, and sudden stops, curves and a bunch of other stuff. Dale also did the same.

The last 3 hours of the day were spent in classroom time and then after that the 50 question written test.

Tomorrow will be more hands on driving followed by the actual driving test.

Oh and I passed the written test!

May 1

We were up at 5 a.m. and out the door by 6 a.m. for breakfast. I must have fallen asleep at 6:30 because I woke up ready to go!

Today's course was even more challenging than yesterday. The entire morning was one drill after another and I just prayed for endurance more than anything.

The instructors were the same ones from the classroom. I feel that their forte is definitely in the outside drills rather than the inside classroom stuff. The classroom lessons were not well structured; but they definitely were on top of the ball with how they ran things outside. I was impressed by this. Also their kind patience.

After lunch came time for the final test. The driving test. Amazingly enough I was not nervous. I was ready to go through it. I felt confident about it. What I was not sure about was if the muscles in my upper arms would get through with me. The more I did a particular exercise drill or the longer I did it, the harder it was to get my muscles to push through.

It was finally over. And in another 15 minutes I was holding my certificate in my hot little hand that says I am now legal to drive a trike! Woooo Hoooo!!!

Another 15 minutes after that and we were heading home. Dale also passed his test, but I knew he would. I had no doubt about him passing.

I felt different coming home than I did on the way over there.

I came away from this Safety course knowing a lot more than when I went in. I came away confident, more knowledgeable about what I could and could not do with my Trike. I just really felt the last day was the turning point in both my knowledge and confidence level.

My competency level is now at an 8!!! If I can get to level 9 I will be happy. To be a level 10 rider in my view is the perfect driver who has had years and years of experience. Dale is a level 10 driver. He's been driving a motorcycle since he was 12. I want to get there but that will take time and lots of practice. Years!

I'm so happy that we traded in my Trike for the Can-Am. It made all the difference in the world. My fibro pain did not flare up once in the whole trip. I felt a muscle ache in my upper shoulder muscle but I could tell that was different from what my Fibro feels like. I am happy. I did it! I can say that for my 59th birthday I passed the test for my motorcycle endorsement! Wow. I did it.

The DMV is closed on Monday but you can bet that Tuesday morning both Dale and I will be at the doors when they open to present our little certificate so they can give us a new driver's license that shows our endorsement for Trike!

May 3

It's a done deal! I have my endorsement on my license! We were up early and within the hour, Dale and I had our new photos taken for our new licenses and the most important part, the line on the back that says I am approved to drive a trike motorcycle!

Now that we have this out of the way we will have to rest for a couple of weeks as we go on to other family matters, but at least we are set. Our new licenses should come in the mail in a few days.

June 3

Ouch! A whole month has passed since we've been able to go out with our trike! We stopped everything to spend a couple of weeks with Dale's mother and her visit to us. Another couple of weeks doing necessary work around the house and keeping an eye on the weather which seems to be very odd for this time of the year. Some days cold and windy and other days, raining cats and dogs.

We finally got a nice day during the memorial weekend and we set out to do a little exploring. It was the first time since the day I got my certificate that I had actually ridden again.

I was worried and nervous that everything I had learned I had forgotten but within the first 5 minutes, it was all there in my mind again, fresh and ready to go. I was very happy.

I drove for the first half of the trip and Dale drove the second half the way home via a different direction. We both enjoyed our ride immensely and came home to plan a summer trip for August when we will take off from our dance lessons. I can't wait!

In the meantime, I have some observations . . .

The similarities between dancing Ballroom and driving a motorcycle!

- Posture! Good posture is needed in both ballroom and driving! Good posture in a dancer is an absolute necessity in Ballroom. The dancer looks elegant, fresh and distinguished as well as he feels better when he is done. Have you ever seen someone slouching when they dance? Shoulders hunched over, butt sticking out, tired looking and definitely unattractive! A motorcycle rider also needs to sit up straight when he drives. Driving in a slouched position can make any driver tired in the first hour of driving and feeling it even more after getting off the motorcycle. Ever notice a policeman on his motorcycle going down the street. Nice upright straight posture. Very sexy!! Yes, posture is very important to both.

- A good motorcycle driver is like a good lead. The lead in Ballroom needs to be totally aware of his surroundings as he navigates the dance floor. A motorcycle driver needs to be aware of his surroundings as well.

- A dancer need to feel the changes in the rhythm (slows and quicks) so he can respond at the appropriate time. A motorcycle driver needs to hear and feel the changes in the rpms as he drives so that he can shift up to the next gear (speed) at the correct time.

- Body positioning is important for a motorcycle driver. He needs to know when and how to lean into the turns. A dancer needs to know proper body position and frame for dancing and how to lead a turn or go into a turn

- A motorcycle driver needs to keep his machine in in good running condition for his own safety. A dancer needs to take care of his body for his own health.

- It's fun to do motorcycle driving with your favorite passenger. It's fun to partner dance with your favorite person!
- Technique is important for a dancer. How you do what you do. The same applies to a motorcycle driver. His technique is a valuable tool.
- The more you dance, the better you get. The more you drive, the more experienced you get. Practice in both crafts is essential.
- When we drive, we dress the part. When we dance we dress the part. Motorcycle Mama . . . Dancing Babe.
- The lead controls how fast his partner and he will dance. The motorcycle rider controls how fast his motorcycle will go.
- Both Ballroom dancing and driving a motorcycle involves mechanics and artistry. One needs to know

the patterns in a dance and how to choreograph the patterns to make a dance happen. One needs to know the mechanics on the proper procedures of driving a motorcycle and in which order in order to make the motorcycle drive correctly. Driving a motorcycle correctly is as much of an art as it is to choreograph a beautiful dance.

- A lead on the dance floor strives to dance seamlessly with his partner as he guides her in a series of turns and glides. A motorcycle rider does the same with his precious motorcycle as he guides her and leans her into turns and seamless glides

- You know you have reached full muscle memory in riding a motorcycle when you can maneuver the motorcycle smoothly and seamlessly, without having to panic about what to do next. You and your motorcycle have bonded and the two of you become as one on the road. It's a sweet ride. The same applies to the Ballroom dancers. When they have their patterns and technique down and memorized and they have finessed it, they dance marvelously together. They flow perfectly. The two dance as one and it's a sweet dance.

- In ballroom there is a certain order that things have to get done in order to master the dance. A motorcycle rider also has a certain order in which things must happen in order to master his driving skills.

- The Ballroom dancer as well as the motorcycle rider must both exercise care and safety in their craft. A careless partner can injure his partner or himself on the dance floor. A careless motorcycle rider can injure himself and others.

- In the same way that a new dancer must be patient with himself as he learns the do's and don'ts to becoming a good dancer, a new motorcycle rider must also be patient with himself as he learns the do's and don'ts of driving.

- Dancers learn a lot of things about other people on the dance floor, i.e. who has good floor etiquette, who knows the basic rules of being a gracious dancer. Motor cycle riders learn a lot about people in cars. i.e. Careless auto drivers or rude auto drivers.

- A motorcycle rider feels the changes in his motorcycle and changes his direction as needed. A follow feels the changes made by her lead partner and she changes and adapts to follow his lead.

- Following the rules of Ballroom and Motorcycle driving makes what you do more fun, easier and safer. Don't pull stunts at either. Someone, if not you will get hurt.

- Booze and dancing or driving don't go together. You need a clear head to drive and have good judgment of the road and although you think you dance better after a couple of drinks to "loosen up" . . . you don't. If you don't want to look or act like a fool . . . . think smart. Hydrate with water, not booze.

One Year Later

I have reached my goal. To get to a 9.5 level of competency. Remember that I said I don't think anyone ever really gets to be a perfect 10 in motorcycling. I don't think anyone is ever done learning. I feel the same about Ballroom Dancing. I don't think we are ever done learning in that arena either. We are always learning something new about ourselves, our partner, our motorcycle and the circumstances of our dance or our ride.

For me; I took on the challenge; I pushed myself not to give up (even though many times I was ready to). I overcame my fears, (and believe me I was terrified!) I have accomplished my goals and I can continue to tell my dance students, don't give up because the more you do it, the better you will get. The more you practice, the more accomplished you will become.

In the last year, we have taken many sweet rides on our Can-Am Spyder Trike. Long rides. Short rides. Dale drove one way and I drove the way back or vice versa. When we are out there I am still amazed at the fact that I am actually driving such a magnificent machine.

I have been dancing all my life. Professionally speaking as Ballroom Dance Instructor for almost 12 years. I am a confident dancer and I am a confident instructor. To all my students, I impart and inject them with my confidence every time we meet. I want them to lose the fear and become confident social dancers.

Parting Words

I am a confident Ballroom dancer. Now I am a confident motorcycle rider. I did it. Thank you for riding with me in this amazing journey.

I leave you with my thoughts for the day.

- Don't wait to enjoy life. Don't wait.
- Don't be afraid to take on a challenge
- It's okay to make mistakes. We become better at what we do when we can learn through our mistakes.
- Be patient with yourself as your teachers are patient with you
- Follow the rules. They are there to help you.

- If you don't like rude people . . . don't be one on the road or on the dance floor
- Each day celebrate your life. Dance, laugh, ride
- Share your passion with someone you love
- When you learn something new, **DON'T** go back in the closet with your new skills otherwise, what was the point of investing the time (and money) to learn?
- Be passionate about life, love and your pursuit of happiness

See you on the dance floor and on the road!